VALERIO MAGRELLI
The Embrace: Selected Poems

Dear Loula-May,

Happy Birthday
my darling.
I hope these words
give you as much
joy as I've found
in them.

My gem was: 'treasure chests that
leak/tired light'.
Big love & fairy-dust
wishes to you

Hannah
x

Valerio Magrelli
The Embrace SELECTED POEMS

TRANSLATED BY *Jamie McKendrick*

faber and faber

First published in 2009
by Faber and Faber Ltd
Bloomsbury House
74–77 Great Russell Street
London WC1B 3DA

Typeset by Faber and Faber Ltd
Printed in England by T. J. International Ltd, Padstow, Cornwall

A CIP record for this book
is available from the British Library

ISBN 978-0-571-25176-6

ACKNOWLEDGEMENTS
I'm grateful to editors of the following reviews and newspapers where some
of these poems first appeared: *Amsterdam Review, London Poetry, London
Review of Books, Modern Poetry in Translation, Poetry* (US), *Poetry Review,
Qualm, Times Literary Supplement, tall lighthouse* and also to BBC Radio 3.
I'd also like to thank both the Rotterdam Poetry International Festival and
the London International Poetry Festival who commissioned the translation
of a number of the poems.

10 9 8 7 6 5 4 3 2 1

Contents

from *Nature e venature* (Natures and Veinings), 1987

from *Esercizi di tiptologia* (Typtological Exercises), 1992

from *Didascalie per la lettura di un giornale*
(Instructions for Reading a Newspaper), 1999

Introduction: VALERIO MAGRELLI

Prosegue il catalogo delle vegetazioni

'The catalogue of vegetation continues' – begins one early poem by Valerio Magrelli. Only some lines later do we realise that the Linnaean impulse behind the poem has thought itself, its own thinking, rather than botany as its subject, but we already sense how the scene of possibly thankless, methodical labour is a wry image for the book he is writing:

> Like a canvas
> much over-painted
> on which many different
> hands have worked . . .

Before its end, this characteristically brief, untitled poem has set in play a series of oppositions: scientific/artistic, solitary/collaborative, internal/external.

Magrelli's remarkable first book, published in 1980 when he was twenty-three, bears the somewhat forbidding title *Ora Serrata Retinae*, which would seem more in the way of an oculist's textbook than a collection of poems. The term signifies the jagged edge, specifically 'the irregular anterior margin of the *pars optica* of the retina'. Each poem in the book is an instrument of perception, with a clear circumference and a scrupulously observed area of concern. They highlight a particular small feature of an internal, often nocturnal, landscape and yet cumulatively they bring a haunting and abundant panorama into view. A demonstrative quality is to the fore – and it's significant that as many as thirteen poems in the book have a 'questo' or 'questa' ('this') in the first line. The poems examine the 'I', as well as the eye that examines. Rhetorically, they also re-configure this infolding movement: 'I think of a tailor / who uses himself as a roll of cloth'. They proceed painstakingly with their 'catalogue of vegetation', describing the moods and torsions of perceiving. Only when they, the poems, have acquired sufficient surety of their own visual and conceptual bias do they gradually and inexorably move outwards.

The book was greeted with quite unprecedented acclaim by many of Italy's most significant writers and received praise from poets as far afield as Octavio Paz and Joseph Brodsky. Not since Eugenio Montale's *Ossi di seppia* has there been such a consensus that here, at last, was a voice inhabited by the whole language and culture, shaping them to its own purposes. Reading them again, a quarter of a century after their publication, what's striking is the sheer nerve of the enterprise: poems scribbled down like diary jottings in a notebook with what looks like a radical economy of means, often a single galvanising metaphor, that focus so resolutely on an aspect of consciousness. The tone is dry and scientific, almost forensic, seemingly hostile to any lyrical effects, and yet again and again, almost despite itself, a fierce concentration propels the poems out beyond the familiar. Elizabeth Bishop's often-quoted letter on Darwin, which praises his outwardly directed 'self-forgetful, perfectly useless concentration', 'sees the lonely young man, his eyes fixed on facts and minute details, sinking or sliding giddily off into the unknown'. Something analogous occurs in these poems with a procedure which is precisely contrary.

The compressed, punning title *Nature e venature* (Natures and Veinatures, or Veinings, 1987) of Magrelli's second volume retains an element of the physiological but places it in a wider landscape. Little could seem further from traditional nature poetry than these curt meditations, and yet they share with a poet like Hopkins an extraordinary impulse not merely to describe but to encompass, almost themselves to perform, the underlying principles of growth and form. Hopkins would be at home within this precisely observed, recursive and inscaped world of veinings, cloud formations, Fibonacci numbers.

[x]

Unlike Hopkins, though, with his flaming palette of 'gold-ver-milion' and 'skies of couple-colour like a brinded cow', Magrelli's poems have the subdued tones of Analytical Cubism or verge on monochrome like Morandi: it's more often as though the world is seen by X-ray or lamplight or moonlight. Even the moonlight has artificial traits, as in his poem 'The moonlight is a work of art . . .' – his coolly irreverent take on an outworn topos.

His third collection is *Esercizi di tiptologia* (1992), 'Typto-logical Exercises'– the word 'typtology' comes from the Greek *typtein*, to beat or batter, and refers to the table-rapping in spiritualist séances and, in Italian, to the language of tapping which prisoners use to communicate. The title marks a shift from the first volume's concern with the visual to acoustic phe-nomena and, by extension, to language itself. 'Exercises' has a musical provenance and is far from the kind of communica-tion we might expect of wall-tapping. The head-on collision in the title between leisure and urgency, between contemplation and need, is a paradox which the poems themselves bear wit-ness to.

All this would seem to make of Magrelli a scholarly, philo-sophical, cerebral poet. And yet the astonishing immediacy of the images and the precision of the language carry an emo-tional charge. A love poem like 'The Embrace' from his third book excavates beneath the domestic, and by way of the cen-tral heating is led to the prospect of millennial destruction on which the frail moment of affection is based. The two flames recall the eerie double flame of Ulysses and Diomedes in Canto xxv of Dante's *Inferno*. This is one example of the way Magrelli's poems quietly situate themselves at the centre of a tradition which they question and qualify. His poems describe the process of their composition and their language keeps measuring its own capacity to observe the world.

Another example can be found in his poem 'Rosebud', whose first line in Italian, '*Non pretendo di dire la parola*' (I do not claim to speak the word) can't fail for an Italian reader to evoke the first line of Montale's famous poem '*Non chiederci la parola che squadra da ogni lato / l'anima nostra informe . . .*' (Don't ask from us the word which squares off on every side / our formless soul . . .). It has the typically Montalian, negative *incipit* and the feel of a manifesto poem, concerned with a possible, and possibly threatened, language. The title alludes to Orson Welles's *Citizen Kane*: 'Rosebud' is what he called his childhood sled but also a sly reference to the name that the newspaper magnate William Randolph Hearst gave to his mistress's vagina. With its sense of the evasiveness of language and its own peculiar, witty self-referentiality the poem moves a fair distance beyond its forebear.

If the technology of the first book was utterly basic – a pencil and a notebook, the present moment of introspection – the third book is populated by current media, the telescreen for example, and the fourth, *Didascalie per la lettura di un giornale*, by the image and sections of a newspaper. *Instructions for Reading a Newspaper* is a long poem in which each of the shorter poems corresponds to a section of the newspaper, such as Games, Horoscopes, Obituaries and so on. The Letters Page is a canny device for allowing entrance to the more personal and lyrical, otherwise excluded. Even the book's title suggests a kind of anti-poetry. The decision for poetry to found itself on the throwaway, the quotidian, the mechanically reproduced, recalls Joyce setting part of his epic *Ulysses* in a newspaper office – with an added, disturbing, almost elegiac touch now that newspapers are no longer our dominant mode of purveying information and news. The poem anatomises an institution, its economics, its way of reproducing reality, and subjects the familiar to an estranging scrutiny. Walter Benjamin's argument that the organisation of newspapers has a way of fragmenting our knowledge of the world is very apt here:

Man's inner concerns do not have their issueless private character by nature. They do so only when he is increasingly unable to assimilate the data of the world around him by way of experience. Newspapers constitute one of many evidences of such an inability. If it were the intention of the press to have the reader assimilate the information as part of his own experience, it would not achieve its purpose. But its intention is just the opposite, and it is achieved: to isolate what happens from the realm in which it could affect the reader. The principles of journalistic information (freshness of the news, brevity, comprehensibility, and, above all, lack of connection between the individual news items) contribute as much to this as does the make-up of the pages and the paper's style.

For all their brevity and their fragmentary style, these poems, as so often in Magrelli, combat that 'lack of connection' which Benjamin intuits. In mimicking a newspaper format, they work in the opposite direction and bristle with connectivity.

The idea of fragments, paradoxically, and of anatomy unites much of Magrelli's poetry. Throughout his work there is an insistence on the corporeal. One poem from his second book describes the extraction of a wisdom tooth (in Italian, *il dente di giudizio*). It is not a simple operation: the tooth has to be worked at, broken into three parts, before it comes free. The tripartite fate of the tooth is mirrored in the three stanzaic divisions of the poem as though in homage to the kind of exact correspondence between poem and thing we encounter in Francis Ponge's work. The relief of sleep at the price of bodily integrity or of wisdom is quietly hinted at, and this kind of unconsoling awareness is often painfully evident in the poems.

But there are other threads to this eleven-line poem which give an odd sacral quality to the object, as though it was both suffering the process of martyrdom and was itself being turned into a holy relic. It is referred to as a sacred fish, it is *segnato* – marked out as a target but also, in the context, signed with stigmata or with the cross – as well as *segato* (*segnato* with an extracted 'n') – sawn, as though it were a particularly luckless saint. Further seams of geological imagery and of artisan vocabulary run through the poem and it's in this context that the slow and freighted movement, the elaboration and unravelling of his language, are utterly essential to the whole design.

As Jonathan Galassi, Montale's translator, remarked of Magrelli, 'his poems are not simply self-referential, but always advance an argument with and about life'. One among many examples is 'Vanishing Point', a poem which tries to imagine how it might be to write a picture like, say, Uccello's *Hunt by Night*, but to inscribe it in the medium of time as opposed to space. This poem is a far cry from the run-of-the-mill picture-poem and an intriguing exploration of how we perceive through language. Its vanishing point, having become a temporal rather than a spatial coordinate, lets us re-think both kinds of composition – the pictorial and poetic.

Magrelli's most recent book, *Disturbi del sistema binario* (Disruptions of the Binary System, 2006) follows and reinforces the tendency of *Instructions for Reading a Newspaper* in making a book of poems an exploration of a unitary (or, in this case, binary) theme. The concerns of the poems range from the domestic to the political, considering notions of doubleness, hybrids and antitheses – its finale is a brilliantly inventive sequence on that visual pun, the *anatra-lepre* (the duck-hare, usually known here as the duck-rabbit), in this case a kind of zoological Jekyll and Hyde. The sequence alternates roman and italic print. The idea of doubleness – and duplicity – so thoroughly explored in this poem has been a feature of Magrelli's world from the start, and can be seen in miniature, though already fully formed, in a early poem such as 'A groove / like the vertical join / in plastic figurines / cuts me in two, two sides, / two slopes . . .', or in the poem on cloning 'Health: Dolly's Eye' in the preceding book.

For all the variety of subject and approach, for all the formidable development from volume to volume, Magrelli's poetry has always had immense cohesion. Whole books can be read as sequences, and frequently the lack of titles for individual poems emphasises this continuity. Tadeusz Różewicz, a poet with whom Magrelli has more in common than he has with most of his Italian contemporaries, speaks of his own 'dogged revision, repetition, returning to the same material and so . . . to the end' as 'the most valuable element' in all his work. In neither poet does this imply a narrowness, but rather a necessary depth and force. I can think of few living poets who have evolved a style so equal to and so inclusive of the most resistant aspects of modernity. A Magrelli poem is equipped to address and carry something back from subjects as various as hijackings, radioactive contamination, dinosaur toys, sheep cloning, recycling, graffiti, skateboarding and environmental destruction. As Marianne Moore said of her ostrich: 'He Digesteth Raw Yron'.

Note on the Translation

The first poem of Magrelli's that I read, some ten years ago, was 'L'abbraccio' ('The Embrace'). My immediate response was such a turbulent mixture of recognition, awe and envy that the only way I could still the chaos was to see if I could write it in English. Besides, I was intensely curious to see if what I admired so much in it might survive the passage. Before this, I'd translated a few Italian poems but with little appetite and mixed results. Turning 'L'abbraccio' into English, I was surprised to discover, actually felt like writing a poem, carried with it the same excitement and pleasure. It seemed to me a fluke, a one-off event, but some years later, in a slightly freer style, I translated his untitled 'Amo i gesti imprecisi' which I called 'The Tic'. For the reader who doesn't have Italian or *the* Italian, it's only fair to note what kind of liberties are taken.

Apart from the addition of a title, there are other deviations. The sentry is given an 'insubordinate eyelid', and forgets what was in the cup where the original is starker. In the last line 'Dentro qualcosa balla', the verb *ballare*, whose usual meaning is 'to dance', in the case of machinery, as here, suggests something clanking or ticking, something out of kilter. My solution 'throbs' may not add up perfectly but it picks up the '*cuore*', the heart, which Magrelli places exactly mid-point in his poem, and contains a sense of longing as well as a hint of physical peril. Magrelli's poem is like a modern, wittily dysfunctional update on that Provençal tradition of the *plazer*, a poem in which writers compile a list of favourite things. For all the departures from the original I feel I haven't betrayed its essential direction.

Another example that might stand for a different kind of making free is my version of 'Parlano' ('They Talk'), which was one of the next that I attempted. Here I have put the unrhymed poem into rhyme – a labour-intensive, counter-intuitive manoeuvre, where more normally in translation it's the reverse that occurs. My excuse for this is that I wanted to intensify the acoustics. With so much at risk of being lost, there has to be the chance of listening out for where a translation might go in the new language, of looking out for what the new language might possibly *add*.

When I had done a dozen or so translations I began to think a whole book might be worth attempting, but it was only about ten years after that first encounter that I set about completing it in a less sporadic fashion. The initial feeling of excitement revived. Where earlier I'd thought of the process as a lucky, random, unrepeatable exchange, I found more and more of his poems elicited a similar engagement – not just petty theft but grand-scale larceny. In other words, what had drawn me in the first instance to a particular poem was latent or lying in wait with the same intensity of recognition in far more poems than I'd expected.

Much theorising about translation is, and has long been, concerned with arguments over the relative claims of domesticating or estranging strategies. Often ignored, where poetry's concerned, are the different kinds of strangeness that poetry itself brings into the equation. Far more interesting than general questions of the differences between two languages is the poem's own divergence from normal use in the original language. The translator must then come to terms with (at least) two different kinds of strangeness. It's probably easier to arrive at some untroubled and consistent-sounding theoretical approach if you know little about the language you're translating from, but, sadly, even an extensive knowledge guarantees practically nothing, except (only perhaps) the absence of gaffes. Aside from the genuinely bilingual and some rarely gifted linguists, however well you know another language it will always remain exterior and opaque in some respects, and poetry, in which that language is paradoxically both most at home and most idiosyncratic, will remain an even more vertiginous challenge. These spots of opacity, though, may have the effect on the foreign translator of heightening attention so that the act of reading is, in more than one sense, an act of listening out. The translator is in the first place a kind of 'listener-out', and then must go on to listen in, must thoroughly absorb what's alien to make it his or her own.

Even here the same problems return. Translating could then become an act of appropriation or, worse, expropriation. Lowell's *Imitations*, which continue to exert an influence today, belong to this *virtuoso* tradition; although their triumphs tend to be most admired by those with little knowledge of the languages and the original poems he was 'imitating'. Elizabeth Bishop, who voiced serious misgivings about *Imitations*, offers an alternative in her translations of the Brazilian poets Carlos Drummond de Andrade and Vinicius de Moraes: a severe adherence to the original which doesn't sacrifice vitality and formal invention. These are just two points along an infinite succession, and they don't represent wholly opposed tendencies anyway – there is no way of miraculously ridding a translation of the translator's voice and limitations. Translators serve the original best by extending the former and coping with the latter as best they can. My own approach has been catholic, pragmatic, even opportunistic, rather than consistent with any theory. I have tried to sense the possibility each poem, with its own peculiar demands, opens up within the new language. I've ditched those (a fair number at that) where I failed to bring over anything new into the English, and any which, on checking later, seemed too close to Anthony Molino's earlier, authoritative translations.

Biographical Note

Valerio Magrelli was born in Rome in 1957. Among many other awards for his poems, he has won the Mondello Prize (1980), the Viareggio (1987), The Easter-Salisburg Prize (1996), the Montale Prize (2002), the Feltrinelli Prize (2002) and the Cetona Prize (2007). A Professor of French literature at the University of Pisa, then Cassino, he has also published critical works on Dadaism, on Paul Valéry and Joseph Joubert, as well as notable translations of Mallarmé, Valéry, Verlaine, Beaumarchais, Roussel and Koltès. He is also the author of two plays and two collections of short prose pieces, *Nel condominio di carne* (2003), a poignant, often witty meditation on his own body and the ills it's heir and host to, and *La Vicevita. Treni e viaggi in treno* (2009), where he records a series of vicarious lives spent travelling by train. He is currently working on a critical study of Baudelaire.

from *Ora Serrata Retinae*, 1980

It's not a glass of water that I keep
beside the bed
but this notebook.
Sometimes I sign words there in the dark
and the following day finds them
dumbstruck and battered by the light.
They're nocturnal things
left out to dry
which wrinkle and burst
in sunlight. Only scattered bits and pieces
remain, faint ceramics of sleep
that overflow the page.
It's the graveyard of the thought
which shapes itself between my hands.

This notebook serves me as a shield,
a trench, a periscope, a loophole.
I look from a dark room into the light;
unseen I see – the spy's furtive tradecraft.
I arrange it so that every line
multiplies like the miracle of the loaves
– a ledger of losses and gains
to reckon up the eras of human commerce.
Surface of flesh on which I scratch
before sleeping, which I caress and knead
like an instep
after the day's hard slog.

Once you brought to the page
the day that had passed, but now
you speak only of speech.
As if in the journey the impression
makes on its way to paper
a chasm had opened.
So moving from one
to the other shore
all the merchandise has been lost
and the traveller,
having forgotten his travels,
can only tell the dangers he's survived.

There's a moment when the body
gathers itself in breathing
and thought stops and hesitates.
Likewise things
tugged by the moon
undergo the influence of
the tidal sigh, the malleable eclipse.
And the boats' planks
swell gently in water.

This page is a room left unoccupied.
Every so often I lug in a broken chair
or a sheaf of journals and drop them
in a corner – and that's it.
Whatever's cast off here, cashiered
from use, settles itself in layers.
It's the last port of call for things
before sinking beneath the house's horizon
in the clear light of their own sunset.

The pen should never leave
the hand that writes.
With time it grows into a bone, a finger.
Fingerlike, it scratches, clutches, points.
It's a branch of thought
and yields its own fruits,
offers shelter and shade.

The white page
like the cornea of an eye.
I hurriedly embroider
an iris and in the iris etch
the deep gorge of the retina.
A gaze then
sprouts from the page
and a chasm gapes
in this yellow notebook.

The pen slips
towards the page's crotch
and the writing silently emerges
in the complex figure
of an African state, in which I arrange
the parallel stripes of sand dunes.
And by this stage I'm drawing
whilst I tell what
being told comes into being.
It's as though a cloud
should have taken on
the shape of a cloud.

Tangled in the bed
are my roots of flesh,
only the head sticks out
like a plant from the earth.
In this exposure to the night
as in a syzygial tide
the light withdraws and unveils
the spirit's fertile nudity.

Sleep subtracts much from life.
The work suspended at the edge of day
gradually sinks into silence.
The mind subtracted from itself
is veiled with eyelids.
And sleep grows within sleep
like a sinister, second body.

At this hour the eye
turns back within itself.
The body wants to shut itself inside the brain
to sleep.
All the limbs rush home.
It's late. And these two girls
seated in the train
lean into their drowsiness,
stunned by sleep.
Animals at pasture.

Summertime, like the cinemas, I shut up shop.
Thought flies off elsewhere and evaporates.
Billboards write white,
the air's warm,
the table weighted with fruit.

This rain of ashes
on the yellow courtyards
makes the sheets
seem gravestones.
Each pegged cloth a shroud
in the vertical noon.

There are some books that serve
to unveil others
but writing's usually about spiriting away,
subtracting certain things from reality
whose loss will then be felt.
This maieutics of the sign
makes them manifest: by their travail
we learn to see them.

Often the page lies becalmed.
It's futile turning it to find
what quarter the wind
might blow from.
Nothing moves.
Thought wavers in that calm.
What navigation wrecked
is there being
painfully repaired.

Stalker

That woman is possessed
of a magic power: she knows
how to do without me.
I'd also like to know
how to do without . . .
But who does she neglect me for?
For what? Intrigued,
I pursue her to uncover
in her hidden love a love
which overpowers my own.
Thus a desire for justice
spurs a man on to a life of crime.

But some internal highway must exist,
a sort of shortcut
between the head and legs
crossing the arms, the stomach
and those parts which in the 18th Book
Homer names the Shameful.
A pathway set apart,
sunk deep into the body,
a vein passed by unobserved
or a navigable waterway,
a network of tramlines
or an underground track. An idea
propped against the wall like an umbrella
and then forgotten.

Ten poems written in one month
isn't that much to show for it
even if this would make the eleventh,
and the themes are not exactly various –
rather there's just the one theme which has
for its theme, as here, the theme.
Which goes to show how much
remains beyond the page,
knocks, but cannot – must not –
gain admittance. Writing's not
a mirror but rather
the shower-screen's frosted glass
– behind which, real enough,
but darkly, a body
is discerned; though whose you couldn't say
only how it moves. So why peer
behind the watermark
when I'm the counterfeiter
and only the watermark's my real work.

Evenings when the light is almost nil,
holed up in bed,
I harvest the mindcast silhouettes
which course across the silence of my limbs.
It's here that I have to embroider
thought's arrass
and spreading out the threads of my self
out of myself design my own figure.
This isn't labour
so much as elaboration.
First of the paper, then of the body.
Drawing forth the forms thought takes,
shaping them according to a measure.
I think of a tailor
who uses himself as a roll of cloth.

My mind is full of women.
Somewhere
the dome of my skull
must be stove in
for such a stream
of murmuring,
such a fountain of love
to enter.
In this shadow land
I roam like a pilgrim
or a monk.
Round every corner,
every curve,
a silent face looks out,
pale as a gravestone.

To write as if this
were a work of translation,
something already penned in another language.
The word is freighted and hesitates,
still keeps vibrating
as when on a keyboard the held notes
endure beyond the detachment of touch,
keep sounding on until their silencing.

The catalogue of vegetation
proceeds.
Here are the shrubs and grasses,
the contrasting species,
thought's botanic refulgence.
Like a canvas
much over-painted
on which many different
hands have worked,
this landscape repeats itself
and assumes the slow
progress of a Gregorian chant.

from *Nature e venature*
(Natures and Veinings), 1987

Fever

lifts me up towards the heat
like a lever
whose fulcrum is
my own
left wrist
– within which are the exact
number of those beats
that overheat me
and make me rise in the night
like a Chinese
paper dragon:
lurid, incandescent

Fibonacci

I note the forehead's curvature
in its utter nakedness
and deduce the same number
which underwrites
how branches grow,
a church's poised façade
the snail-shell spiral
and the form of leaves.

I've often imagined that looks
outlive the act of seeing
as though they were poles
with measurable trajectories, lances
hurled in a battle.
Then I think that in a room
just left lines
of this kind must stay
for some time poised
criss-cross, cross-hatched,
upholding their structure
like pick-up-sticks.

A boat is a lever, and nothing's lovelier than a boat.
– Simone Weil

A flying city, self-propelled,
poised upon a forest
of stakes, moving in accord
with the enchantment
of its own weight, with the grace
of its distribution,
leaning,
wavering in a faint tremor, a friction
that will erode it. All along its canals
laden with fruits, with fruit salads,
pass boats whose keels are skewed like
spinal columns, twisted
by water, out of kilter,
barely managing to balance.

And the crack in the teacup opens
A lane to the land of the dead.
– W. H. Auden

. . . as when a crack appears
the length of a cup.
– R. M. Rilke

You gave me this red cup
from which to drink to my days on earth
one by one
in the pallid mornings, the pearls
strung on thirst's long necklace.
And should it fall and crack,
stunned by regret,
I'll have to mend it
so as to keep unbroken
that sequence of kisses.
And each time the round
of handle or rim
chips, I'll glue it back
until my love
has finished
the slow hard graft of a mosaic.

Right down the dip of the cup's white slope,
along the clear curved inside,
like a jag of lightning,
fixed and black,
the crack descends
– sign of a storm
whose thunder still echoes
over this landscape
of glazed resonance.

Antaura was the Neoplatonic name for the accursed
and diabolic demon of the migraine.
– A. A. Barb

Drum rolls from the depths,
from night's hemisphere,
herald the migraine.
Tribes, constellations
break out, their crests rear up
with the plumed tail
of the beast from below
while the world's inner walls
clang and resound,
hollowed out, percussive,
a living eardrum.

If I have to use digits to call you,
you undergo a transformation
into digits, your lineaments mutate
to the number that gets through to you.
The double three,
then the nine that comes third
recall something in your face.
When in search of you
I have to draw up your figure,
I have to spawn the seven ciphers
that are analogues of your name
until the combination safe
of your living voice
unlocks itself.

All of a sudden, while I'm on the phone,
some static rucks our voices,
multiplies them, springs open a long view
within hearing's
dark space.
I catch an image of myself vertical, a sleepwalker
suspended above a fugue of voices,
twin sisters, bound one to the other,
stunned by the contact.
I hear the tongue of the ancient creature
from the underworld,
the hideous, braided words and phrases,
the monster who,
misshapen, many-headed, calls me
from the deep.

In children's drawings
the violence of the lines
is what's striking. The mind seems
to have grown crooked,
carried away by the crayon.
Everything's forever twisted
or perhaps only bent
as when dipping in water
the oar appears broken.

The toy stands out,
has left the game to show itself
alien to the alien.
Even childhood returns
hostile, altered,
like someone else's.
Its traces belong
to itself alone,
to the fossil nature of the child.

I should like, one day,
to be turned to marble,
to be stripped of nerves,
glistening tendons, veins.
Just to be airy enamel,
slaked lime, the striped
tunic of a wind
ground to a halt.

A groove
like the vertical join
in plastic figurines
cuts me in two, two sides,
two slopes. One side moves
instinctively – a natural –
guided by impulse, being just
that: the felicitous act.
The other's hopeless,
an invalid that suffers
without ever recovering:
a convalescent space.
Punishments have been devised
where the live person is tied
to a corpse, though not
in that case
his own corpse. So
this paralysis that strikes
one half of the body
would seem to explain
the soul's angle of inclination,
its gradient and overhang.

How many tunes, heard once only,
which follow their own promptings,
which we can't get out of our heads,
which furrow the space there. In the wood
of violins X-rays show up
the intricate damage,
a snaky, shifting, threaded
coiffure rayed out with veins
that weave across and excavate
the fibrous interior.
So worm-eaten with music,
we become light-headed, empty-headed,
as if made of fine lace.

They belong to no one,
the balconies of blocks of flats.
Washing is left out
there to dry like
linen in the desert.
They're highland planes,
vast uninhabited zones,
left to fend for themselves
in their aerial infancy.

Rosebud

I make no claim to speak the word
which shot from the heart can travel through
the twelve pierced axes
before it strikes the suitor's heart.
I trace my target out
in a circle round the object struck.
I make my mark out of the mark I've made:
whatever I hit. – I cheat,
choosing the bull's eye after the shot's fired
and as though handling a faulty weapon
of which by this stage
I know the exact degree
of deviation, now
I have the sight in my sights.

Having nothing to write
causes that same boundless
childlike foreboding
as being unable to find
a bed abroad.
You look high and low
but every room's already booked.
You try elsewhere but meanwhile
it's got late and there's no
hint or hope of an opening.
So where are we going to stay the night?

On the beach, rotten wood, tyres, bottles,
sodden stuff – all things bust
and putrefied – I love them all:
what's washed up, spewed out, good for nothing,
what no one wants
to have or filch.
In April the air
takes on a hint of warmth.
Glows like a cheek.

You stand on a pier
as though on a ruin,
a bridge that gives
onto the waters.

Interrupted sleep whistles and creaks,
a snapped branch that bares
green virgin wood – it's broken clean
but the sundered parts remain
held together
by a long white fibre,
meek, shivering, undefended,
the plant's heart and soul,
its tendon.

With the passage of time all the milk
goes bad, as though
it had turned evil.
It contracts, solidifies,
sloughs off its proper liquid form,
assumes a body, revived
in new compact flesh, extracted
from the beast. It turns to
cheese, a metamorphosis
into an occult creature, the dead
fruit off a living plant,
a pale sated lunar being.

The moonlight is a work of art,
a substance first outlined then polished
till it's flint stone, mineral flame,
but flame that's enfeebled, dead, like grass
grown in the dark,
a pale, ritual vetch
whose glow has the cold
submerged phosphorescence
of acetylene.

With cogs, tiny levers and teeth
the clock seems a chariot armed with scythes
to rip the day to bits – it rends
the day's corpse, tears its joints and tendons,
shreds the hours, bones them, as night's
rotation uproots
the sky's light and strips bare
numbers, figures, frameworks,
the shining cloudy skeleton
of the constellations.
So, X-rayed, the body
retires, at low tide,
uncovers its bed, the underlying
lowlands, the mountain tops,
the dormant fossils
beneath light's healthy flesh tones.

German

How sad it is to learn a language too late.
They've shut the doors,
and you're left outside with a small
broken piece in your hand. You ask
what's it for, how it works, if it's well
made, but it's no use knowing things
one by one. What's missing is
the casting, the pressure, the fire.
And you only meet
words you don't know
or have already forgotten.
I have this fear that German's lost
the nouns and verbs I have by rote.
Perhaps I'm the fault, the breach
that gapes within its dictionaries.

Because it won't come out whole,
a sacred fish, enamelled, all aglow,
it won't come out at all.

It has to be divided, scored, crossed,
worked on, keeping its nerve
intact, its vein shining
in a night of stone.

Now I can sleep –
rid of the wisdom tooth,
that's sawn into three parts,
pulled piece by piece,
broken down to be uprooted.

The Tic

Gestures that go astray
appeal to me – the one
who trips up or upturns
a glass of . . . the one who forgets,
is miles away, the sentry
with the insubordinate eyelid
– my heart goes out
to all of them, all who betray
the unmistakable
whirr and clunk
of the bust contraption.
Things that work are muffled
and mute – their parts just move.
Here instead the gadgetry,
the mesh of cogs, has given up
the ghost – a bit sticks out,
breaks off, declares itself.
Inside something throbs.

Vanishing Point

Which is the left-hand side of the word?
How does it move about in space?
Where does it throw its shadow
(and can a word cast shadow)?
How can it be observed from behind
or set against the recession of space?
I should like to render in poetry
the equivalent of perspective in painting.
To give a poem the depth of a rabbit
escaping through the fields and make it
distant whilst already
it speeds away from the one who's watching
and veers towards the frame
becoming smaller all the time
and never budging an inch.
The countryside observes
and disposes itself around the creature,
around a point that's vanishing.

On one street they fashioned coloured busts of saints
in every size whilst on another
only arms and painted candles, faces
boxed in cramped frames; elsewhere
they drew scenes of people
saved from drowning, with white clouds
to write a message on, or else they worked
on hearts of beaten silver
rayed out with fine spokes,
every part of the body turned into jewels,
prosthetics, corpus delicti
to start proceedings
in the streets and courts of heaven.

This writing's being worn away,
its angles smoothed, the 'r's,
the 'm's, are turned
and sanded down and roll like stones
the currents shift from shore to shore.
Faces also,
faces waste away
from the pressure of being watched.
They turn into a landscape
full of ruins.

My heart's been chipped,
its hard enamelled surface nicked
and keyed – that coat of light,
cold and metallised, was frail:
the product and effect
of fired paint.

*

I'm solitary as a nail
nailed to its shadow,
lone as a bullet
which hasn't time
to cast a shadow.

*

Hurtling through the air
at over a hundred,
barely touching
the things
I pass over
but already too far,
too far on to hear
the noise they make
as they collapse.

Asphalt Jungle

They rove through the night –
these now huge buses,
souls in torment,
treasure chests that leak
tired light,
trembling, empty, useful
only to those
way off, at a far remove;
back and forth they rove
forever bound
to a line
of grief,
at every stop
delivered of
a sigh
that seems a prayer.

Sighs and smiles on the telephone
ask no reply
– it's the voice that shines forth,
that counts,
that, tinkling, greets
and holds out for a fair exchange
the way that money's turned
to foreign currency.

The telephone is my tap,
fountain of voices, shower.
The water's always the same
but each drop's
distinct. Think of the poor
carbon grains
that dance a different
dance with every breath
renewed – the winged ones, the sparrows
that hop around this bird bath
just because we're talking.

Whilst I'm walking I smoke
and with each toke I take
I cleave through my smoke
to arrive where I wasn't
myself yet present
where my smoke had been sent.

from *Esercizi di tiptologia*
(Typtological Exercises), 1992

That matter engenders contagion
if interfered with in its deepest fibres
cut out from its mother like a veal calf
like the pig from its own heart
screaming at the sight of its torn entrails;

That this destruction generates
the same energy that blazes out
when society turns on itself, the temple's veil torn
and the king's head axed from the body of the state
until the faith healer becomes the wound;

That the hearth's embrace is radiation
nature's pyre which unravels
helplessly before the smiling company
so as to effect the slightest increase
of the surrounding temperature;

That the form of every production implies
breaking and entry, fission, a final leavetaking
and that history is the act of combustion
and the Earth a tender stockpile of firewood
left out to dry in the sun,

is hard to credit is it not?

Xochimilco

I build myself upon an absent column
– Henri Michaux

Bindings, bandages, plants' beards
waft downwards to the depths,
unite themselves with the soft,
the blind, the untouched,
echo-located abyss,
unite themselves with me.
Out of reeds is this earth made
– rafts, their bindings loosed, tongues
wagging to the pulse of wavelets.
My founding was ritual,
insentient – I spired from
a landspill, was born
from an ache, a lack;
pile-works, pick-up-sticks, interstices,
a stake stuck in the void.

Aperçu

Only the mad excrescence . . .
– Osip Mandelstam

The tapeworm, the parasite,
the scrounger, the saprophyte,
cancer: they're born from organisms
which conceal their own ends
like the music of the West.
First the budding
of timid dissonance, then the metastases
which invade the sonorous body and break it down,
admirable corruption and orchard
of death. It's the history of a tonal catastrophe,
arrhythmic cells, superfetations,
or else of a Hijacker (and cancer
always hijacks its own vehicle).
And here's the Earth, poor aircraft
taken hostage by an armed passenger.

Heligoland

A stone slab immersed and gently tilted
towards the UK, a launch pad
of brightest green, warren and U-boat den,
riddled, hollowed out, island and concealed arsenal.
Then, defeated, it must be cancelled out, rubbed off
the atlas like a silver scratch-card scraped by a coin
to see if we'll win something. TNT
roars for months in the cave of winter, blows
across the North Sea, within and under, till the village
is sawn in half. Now on the brand-new profile
of the rockscape (freshly minted in the sheer
excitement of this shoreline bricolage) its history
is inscribed in the exposed layers. Beneath the grass,
some kitchen tiles, asphalt, a sitting room,
strands of sprangled wires, furnish a fitting
anatomy lesson in the open air, open
to the four winds.
But the plan ground to a halt, and where explosives failed
tourism succeeded. And here they are – the standard string
of duty-free shops, the island a market,
worm-eaten, sand-blasted and manhandled into
the shape of a chair that limps, a spent projectile aka
SHELL CASE,
a dented disc left to float
among the thousand medal-souvenirs.

They Talk

Such is the silence that one can hear the tinkle
of a teaspoon falling in Finland.
– Josef Brodsky

But why's it always behind my walls?
Always there, the voices, always
when night falls
they start to talk. They bark. Or even think
whispering's better. (Whilst I can feel their
words become this thread of air
that chills me and chokes me and breaks
my sleep up). At the polar circle's brink
a couple wept together in their room,
beyond a wall they wept
– its luminous membrane
tender as a drumskin
or an eardrum.
(Whilst I resounded – the sound box
of their story.) Till they started in on
the roof at my place, the whole thing, the guttering,
battering away at the front, the back,
the top, the bottom, always battering
and chattering away together only when I slept,
only because I slept,
only because I was always
the sound box
of their stories.

On the Name of a CUV from the GDR
which in German Means 'Satellite'

Satellites of a solar system which is falling apart,
of a nucleus that disintegrates in free particles
and loses its pearls from the strings of orbital masses, stones
of a hailstorm which, ticking,
shines on the asphalted West:
TRABANTS – pink, beige and pastel
green, two-stroke tin-tubs, tinkling
pale-blue jalopies, trembling trines,
'*Trabis*', portable nations, knick-knacks
of a fossilised and stylised class,
little tin cans in which are stashed
a fearful and meek Communist bourgeoisie, mineral
exhibits, Mickey Mouse car
in flight from your paid killer of a pied piper,

welcome to Hamlyn, BRD!

Porta Westfalica

One cloudy day, at Minden,
in a taxi that takes me
in search of these two words.
I ask around and no one knows
what they stand for – my point exactly, I reply –
what kind of place is it and where, and whether
fortress or lock. Still, the name shines
on the map, emits a blaze in the tight knot
of consonants that give off short
luminous vowels like the weapon
of a man lying in wait in the wood.
He gives himself away and I go to hunt him down.
The Op Art panorama opens up between trees
and waters, whilst the signs point out now
a tower of Bismarck, now William's mausoleum,
the statue with its left leg emblazoned
by the words: 'Manuel war da',
chiselled maybe with his house keys, a tenuous
gold thread on the bronze's verdigris,
the sinuous line of the signature, a river
among rivers. I leave the car and start to walk.
Dead leaves, shifting light and frozen air.
The pang of a twisted ankle. I am
a spinning top, a screw
that's been unscrewed. There's nothing else.
Yet here is the sign, here the earth
throttles itself, here is the bypass, the wall
of a watery Berlin in the midst of
phreatic strata, man-made basins,
war and peace and the Latin language.
Nothing. And wandering in the forest, I think
of the driver who waits and frets,

of the driver who waits and frets
and takes this opportunity to clean the car windows
whilst with a chittering sound
under the dashboard the meter runs on
like a brook, the propeller of money,
dyke, conduit pipe, outlet, opened lock, aorta,
haemorrhage of time and mitral valve,
Porta Westfalica of my life.

Potential Energy

The long drive over,
I stare ahead
at the face of this person
I'm talking to.
And the features peel
apart on either side
– a tree-lined boulevard –
in one continuous
opening out of space.
You be my street!
And when you start
to talk I just
keep hurtling on
through pure
unobstructed
miles of face.

The Embrace

As you lie beside me I edge closer
taking sleep from your lips
as one wick draws flame from another.
And two night-lights are lit
as the flame takes and sleep passes
between us. But as it passes
the boiler in the basement shudders:
down there a fossil nature burns,
down in the depths prehistory's
sunken fermented peats blaze up
and slither through my radiator.
Wreathed in a dark halo of oil,
the bedroom is a close nest
heated by organic deposits,
by log pyres, leafmash, seething resins . . .
And we are the wicks, the two tongues
flickering on that single Palaeozoic torch.

Removals Man

What is translation? On a platter
the pale and glaring head of a poet.
– Vladimir Nabokov

The weighed-down removals man
who empties my room
does the same work as me.
I too arrange house removals
for words, for words
which aren't mine,
and lay hands on
what's beyond me
without quite figuring out
what it is I'm moving.
I am moving myself,
translating the past into a present
which travels sealed
and folded in pages
or in boxes labelled FRAGILE
about whose contents I can only guess.
And this is the future, the shuttle
moving back and forth, the metaphor,
labourer time, time with its hither zone,
its middle west or east,
transfer and trope,
the removals firm.

I was lying on an outpatient's bed
hidden behind a screen.
'Antigone', 'Yes', 'You there?', 'Yes, here.'
The bones of the back, the backbone.
And they start talking to each other,
the two old folk, the two old voices.
Because a voice grows old,
even in sounds you find the bone of time,
even in breathing. They sighed and inside
the sound, the sound echoed itself,
an echo preceding the words themselves.
Something wrecked and unhinged, the marrow
stripped from the spinal column and
unsheathed like a glittering sword,
voice-carcass,
backbone of the voice

Lesson in Metrics

A steel comb unpicks
the notes and trickles
a music like threads
of candyfloss. Like
a snake-charmer, charmed
himself, I fall under the spell
of the tongue of sound
which unravels while
the teeth of metal,
the rosary of hooks,
rips this flesh in strips
and the listener's heart
is flayed.
It's my heart they're playing here!
Syrup and stench. When the outside
with the ballerina's broken,
the music box stops dead
because bad taste requires
its own fine tuning,
the jewel case for the wild pearl
of affectation. Night falls.
Frankenstein's violin calls me.
And I'm that musical monster
condemned to the musical wheel
of his musical nostalgia.

from *Didascalie per la lettura di un giornale*
(Instructions for Reading a Newspaper), 1999

Date

It begins here:
light of a dead star
that has reached us from the pluperfect present.
Its today is yesterday, corpse-light,
the memory trace of a daily afterlife.

Price

Inscribed on the temple's pediment
it unfurls itself in *lire* and the broad
frieze of foreign currencies.
Print for print, paper money
serves for the acquisition of a money paper
whose magic value runs out in 24 hours
when at midnight the flaming
carriage of the very latest turns
back into a pumpkin, expired news,
money out of circulation, wastepaper,
carcass of reports and updates,
carrion already picked clean.

Bar Code

Let us honour the topmost banner
fluttering over the kingdom of commodities
– the encoded soul of price,
rose of the name and name of the rose,
bundle of stems, fasces
of tendons and veins
– wrist on which to take
the pulse of money.

Daily Saint

That name that lies alongside
the day of the daily bears
the memory of a lacerated corpse.
There's always some bishop, martyr or virgin
to stain with sacred blood the fruit of
the rotaries – not olives
but printer's ink under the press.

From Our Correspondent in:
Theatre Square, Dresden

Don't let's hang about
on the cobblestones.
The equestrian statue – keep
going – represents the king.
Yes, the Dante translator.
Now let's move on.
Lovely theatre, first rate, but
no point in dawdling
because this paving's contaminated
(a nuclear accident
near the quarry) and here we are
already like ghosts on this X-ray plate, like ghouls,
radiological tourists, little glass vessels
blown with a breeze of electrons.

Readers' Letters: First Encounters

Suddenly I saw a hummingbird, or rather
I heard it whirring among the branches
of a bush I was rummaging through.
Or better still, I became aware of its trembling
like the hiss
of a hundred thousand volts
along power lines strung from pylon to pylon
across our countryside – little birds of pure energy.
And this pure source was the same that,
hidden, whirls
in particle accelerators
along the blind wedding of an underground circuit.
Or perhaps marriage
is the structure which stores the power
consigning it to an annular course
at the same time mobile and static
(the aureole of sex). And yet in the shock
I experienced at the threat of its freedom,
freedom to strike me, the hummingbird came first,
preceded every other form – it was the lightning flash
which has still to choose the track it burns through
and so was every possible track.
The power of an unbearable crash –
he was the cascade I'd gone in search of
as I went on rummaging through those bushes.

Photography

It's that the flash cuts the umbilical cord
of the light. It cuts, that pair of scissors,
the slow long filament of the
gaze, the long intestine
which feeds us; it cuts in two
because the image
comes into the world separating itself
from its mother.
And that pupa of shadow,
that cocoon, is the basket
left to rock upon the waters
to rescue form and keep it safe.

Poetry

Poems always have to be re-read,
read, re-read, read again, re-charged;
every reading energises them –
they're machines to re-charge sense
and meanings gather in them, a buzz
of particles that lie in wait,
withheld sighs, clicking and ticking
inside the Trojan horse.

Our City: Graffiti

Where does this foetal, feral language
come from, with its shimmering
alpha-numerical tags?
Who speaks this spray-on Esperanto
from walls, trams and entry-phones?
What is it telling us,
this crackly static tongue
that calls from the deep?

Our City: Landscape with Skateboards

To play on monuments, to make them sound,
they turn stairways into keyboards,
from railings and ramps extracting
heraldic arpeggios
and gliding, glissando, at such length
they wear themselves out, this excluded
brotherhood of music
with their coded manners
and wounded integrity,
their tribal, adolescent dandyism.

Children's Corner: Lullaby of the Gobi

The desert breathes on the Celestial Empire.
The Emperor of China is cold.

To warm him up again his subjects give him
an interminable scarf
of stone.

And if this gift proves useless
in stemming the cold wind off the steppes
at least it shall be a sign of the Earth
– from the Moon its one and only sign.

Children's Corner:
Aid Association for Asthma Sufferers

Don't be afraid of breathing,
because it gives and takes like the tide:

let it go free without grabbing hold of it,
don't shut it in the dark well of apnea.

Be indulgent with breathing,
as if it were an invisible yo-yo:

if rustling it should vanish and desert you,
still rustling always it returns.

Games: Chess

White to play
and mate in three moves.
We never know which.

Games: Rebus

A world without time.
Without a breeze.
Everything is still
and exhaustingly full of meaning.
There's no end of meaning and sheer slog
in this worksite of sense.
Every word is a gravelly road-bed
of letters and figures.
Everything weighs a ton.

The Interview

With an IQ of 154
the actress interviewed
boasts of belonging
to Mensa. Beyond
count are the hypotheses
on the source of that scar
she wears on her neck
(a whole internet site
is dedicated to the burning question).
Body and soul are mere
sheathings, the stuff of
cryptic legends, but where,
where is that third language
to grasp your being, star,
to transform you, Sharon
into Rosetta Stone.

Cartoons

You should know that thought is smoke,
cartoon bubbles
like an Injun smoke signal
on the heights
and that the word breathed out
from the lips is pneuma
in the blown Murano glass
flask of the voice.

Review Page

Wedged between finance and films,
padded room of a philological
stammer, wafted ribbon of seaweed
jinking in the critical aquarium,
it still holds out . . . an impinged-on space
and, you'd say, mute ostentorium
if it weren't for the whisper
of those tiny bubbles that rise
(expelled oxygenated syllables)
from a hidden motor,
fountain of breathing,
book-propeller.

The Boundary

The boundary between my life and another's death
passes through the sofa in front of the TV,
a pious shoreline where we receive
our daily bread of horror.
Faced with the sublime injustice
which has dragged us ashore to let us
contemplate the shipwreck, to be just
represents the minimum coin
of decency we can bestow on ourselves,
beggars of sense,
and on the god who with impunity
has made us comfortable on dry land,
on the right side of the screen.

To Let: Unfurnished

Small house to rent overlooking the railway
with a basement area
next to the bus terminal
and drawing room adjoining the Underground.
Noise is at home in the houses of the poor
where small isolated families
huddle together – little birds perched on
high-tension wires, the high
tension of wealth and class,
of cash flow;
that invisible shock
which divides the cows
in the fields, and you from us.
Don't touch the current that flows beside you,
leave it to sigh between pylons,
rumbling along the power lines
in its coppery
braided stream.

Health: Dolly's Eye

Et pour des visions écrasant son oeil darne
– A. Rimbaud

Note: *Up until the last century, in northern France, the dialect*
term darne *meant 'afflicted by giddiness, vertigo'. Used mainly for*
sheep, the adjective could also be applied to people.

Whilst we celebrate the fiftieth anniversary
of the Universal Declaration of Human Rights
synthetic sheep proliferate.
The first one's name was 'Dolly',
from the Greek 'Dorothea'. Gift of God?
– Ripped from him, rather: prototypical,
god-repellent creature.
See how the cloned one dwells within her,
leaks through her looks. She's there
like a mirage, a double, a vicarious body,
a shadow expecting the return
of someone.
She's the woolly ambler stalled
at a fork in the road of the breed.

from *Disturbi del sistema binario*
(Disruptions of the Binary System), 2006

The Shadow

Sunday morning
I'm woken by my daughter's voice
who shouting
asks her brother
if it's true the Bomb
when it explodes
leaves the shadow
of man on the wall.
(Not of 'a man'
but 'of man' she says.) He
agrees that it does.
I turn in my bed.

The Duck-Hare Individual

I point to a particular spot and say:
'This is the eye of the hare or the duck.'
But in this drawing how can something be an eye?
– L. Wittgenstein

Innocence

This is the secret of the duck-hare:
to be guilty as hell whilst taking care
to preserve one's innocence.

Optical

How come all this time
I've been staring at a picture of the duck
never once seeing hide nor hair
of the hare?
I was trying to unravel the concept of deceit
in moral terms when I was merely
the dupe of a visual pun.
I'd opted for the ethical
when the problem was optical.

Really They Halve It

Dual beings populate the earth.
It seems as though they double it
though really they halve it.

The Hare Always Comes in Second

According to a law of perception
no one can see the duck and the hare
at once. Either one or the other;
and one after the other.
But biographical prevails over graphical reality
and asserts a further rule:
like the blade of the sword-stick
the hare always comes in second.

To the Enemy's Sun

We ripen in the sun of injustice.
In the sun of hostility, we ripen.
We're leavened by the heat of the offence,
for the offence is the breath, the force,
which conveys us into the oven
where we'll all be turned into bread.
The wheat swells, weighs, bends the weak stalk.
The golden harvest bends its head to the enemy's sun.

Who Looks the Other Way

Question: And what happens when
a duck-hare looks into the mirror?
Who does he see? Or rather,
given that the duck is first to appear
does he see his second profile emerging?
Is he aware of being a dual creature?
Unfortunately not. As, thanks to a
convenient neurological switch,
there's no connection between the two halves:
Jekyll and Iago only live in fables.
These kinds of monsters disown
their monstrous side
so no acknowledgement occurs.
The cruelty of the duck belongs to the hare
who, not by chance, looks the other way.

I Had Nothing to Do with It!

The sense of guilt is a lit match
that moves from hand to hand, in a circle,
ever more rapidly.
Quick! Quick! It's about to go out
and it had better not end with me –
I had nothing to do with it!

Dual

As they go on, becoming ever more distant from themselves,
they lose all consciousness of their own identities.
– M. Terestchenko

Could we say then that this kind of duck
is actually possessed by the hare?
Yes, but if that were so, how could
the individual be held to account?
That's the point, in this case the individual is dual.

About an Infected Substance

It's pointless trying to decontaminate
tower blocks lagged with asbestos:
better demolish them, and start from scratch.
How am I supposed to rid myself of rage,
this wire-wool, fine dust
of highly toxic stuff
I'm made of, this avalanche
of foul fibres that compose me,
a stuffed creature,
my skin sewn round a lethal mass,
the merest cladding of film
about an infected substance.

Of Doubleness

What does the animated cartoon think of
when his fellow-creature holds forth?
He presents a fixed empty gaze, gaze of an animal
(*weltarm*, 'poor-in-world', the philosopher calls it).
And what is the duck-hare thinking of?
As for worlds, he owns two of them.
So which does he live in with his two-room mind?
Perhaps they're rented out
and that's the root of doubleness.

Rubbish Dump

Piles of recycled material
(or at best regenerated).
Bricks made of faeces and of mud.
A cup fashioned from a tin can,
a plastic pullover
are fine, but lampshades
made of human skin
are something else. This is the far
limit established by the group.
Trinkets made from kidney stones?
OK if they're your own. Poetry.
The rubbish dump.

He Turns His Head Away

One day I tried this experiment:
of putting the duck in front of
what the hare had committed
and holding it there.
It was like putting a nail in the plug:
a flash, then the lights go out.
He refused. I tried again. The same happened.
There's a short circuit in such designs
which bars any way through
from one to the other side of the perspective.
Because of this some hares are capable
of making lampshades of human skin
whilst the duck, unaware,
turns his head away.

I Keep Them Out

Wasp-voices hum and buzz
in a stinging swarm
that bumps against my window panes:
they want in, but I keep them out.

For Burying the Corpses

> *To the lynxes of discourse are counterposed the cuttlefish*
> *of the soul.*
> – B. Gracián

> [. . .] *No sooner are the doors of the soul opened wide than*
> *the beasts emerge from the den of the heart.*
> – G. Mazzarino

Far from the beast, here there's only a hare.
But it all comes down to the fact
dissimulation happens unbeknownst.
They intrigue me, these Sleepwalkers of Evil.
(Another interpretation:
the two sides of the face sleep in alternate phases,
and the one doesn't even dream
of the other's existence.)
The duck is unaware of his better half,
the other side of the psychic moon,
the little garden back of the house
for burying the corpses in.

Heart Lesions

But can the figure really be accused
of having turned its face away,
of being two-faced? How could it
when it's always worn two expressions?
Surely the ambiguity lies with the beholder.
We're dealing with a defect of the gaze
which causes lesions in the heart.

Sharp Little Teeth?

> *The patient would frequently, especially when shaving, question*
> *whether the face staring at him from the mirror was really his own,*
> *and even though he knew it could be physically no other, on several*
> *occasions he found himself grimacing or sticking out his tongue*
> *'just to be sure'.*
> – D. Macrae and E. Trolle

Perhaps it's only a problem of agnosia,
when, that is, the subject's not in a position
to recognise an aspect of himself.
They seem criminals, but they're like mental patients
who mistake their own image
for that of a stranger.
Narcissus reversed:
if the Greek hero took himself for another,
the patient, on the contrary, discerns the other
in place of himself.
What a lovely yellow beak I have
but whose are those sharp little teeth?

Morality's Siding

There are two ways of denying the evidence:
to shut one's eyes or else
avert one's gaze.
Sometimes though a third way is provided:
it's quite sufficient that the spectacle
takes place elsewhere.
If the duck can stare serenely at the injustice
he's involved in, that's because the image,
by way of the pupil, changes track
and arrives in the hare's brain
shunted on the dead rail
into morality's siding.

The Calm Surface?

The Word skims the water and tots up
as many as a dozen leaps and bounds.
Hats off! But what does the calm surface
know of the dark below?

Horror

That's the error:
to imagine the solution lies
in things being mysteriously vertical,
in the heart of the water the stone skims over.
But there's nothing in the deep,
no third dimension exists:
everything's played out on the same plane,
or rather in the self-same figure!
You just have to look at him in a different way.
Flatland.
I'd speak of the unconscious being on the self-same plane –
for me, the plane of horror.

Indifference

> *Hardly finding a free corner within their conscience.*
> – F.-R. de Chateaubriand

I've come to a conclusion:
Evil needs room.
You can't do everything at home.
You need an alter ego, an alias, a double,
at the least a meta-me –
the mummified Mummy in *Psycho*.
You need the hare, the delegate beast,
a portable scapegoat
to bear the weight of the crime.
It's just a question of cubic capacity:
of finding room for indifference.

Post Script: Goodbye to Language

i

Suddenly one 6th January some years ago,
I met my black Epiphany,
when the hare leapt before my eyes
and replied whilst I was speaking to the duck.
Till then I'd blindly believed
in the sacred liturgy of conversation.
To communicate, for me, had meant a joint endeavour
– the communion of the common word.
That day I understood the Janus-animal's intent
to sabotage, or Janify, each verbal exchange.
Now I live in a world of ultra-bodies
where anyone might reveal a hidden profile,
a parallel self,
unknown even to the self itself.

ii

It was a bitter *Befana**
which closed my millennium.
Instead of bearing gifts
she took away what I held most dear:
the dream of a shared language.

Forked creatures, immune to the word,
loomed before me,
and were invulnerable to the truth.
I had entered the age of the duck-hare,
the era of iron, of silence.

* *La Befana* is an ugly old woman who brings Italian children presents
(traditionally candy for good behaviour, coal for bad) on Epiphany, January
6th. Her name is thought to be derived from the Greek *epiphaneia*.